The Camp of Philosophy

By William Bloomfield

Copyright © 2021 Lamp of Trismegistus. All rights reserved. No part of this publication may be reproduced or transmitted in any form or by any means, electronic or mechanical, including photocopying, recording, or by any information storage and retrieval system, without permission in writing from Lamp of Trismegistus. Reviewers may quote brief passages.

ISBN: 978-1-63118-580-9

Esoteric Classics:
Studies in Alchemy

Other Books in this Series and Related Titles

The Secret Book of the Philosopher's Stone by Artephius (978-1-63118-517-5)

Book of Vexations by Paracelsus (978-1-63118-520-5)

Hermetic Arcanum by Jean d'Espagnet (978-1-63118-519-9)

Aurora of the Philosophers by Paracelsus (978-1-63118-507-6)

Rosicrucian Rules, Secret Signs, Codes and Symbols by various (978-1-63118-488-8)

On the Philadelphian Gold by Philochrysus & Philadelphus (978-1-63118-511-3)

Paracelsus, the Four Elements and Their Spirits by M P Hall (978-1-63118-400-0)

The Stone of the Philosophers by A E Waite (978-1-63118-509-0)

Freher's Process in the Philosophical Work by D A Freher (978-1-63118-484-0)

The Rosicrucian Chemical Marriage by Christian Rosenkreuz (978-1-63118-458-1)

The Alchemical Catechism of Paracelsus by Paracelsus (978-1-63118-513-7)

Alchemy in the Nineteenth Century by Helena P. Blavatsky (978-1-63118-446-8)

Rosicrucians and Speculative Masonry in the Seventeenth Century (978-1-63118-489-5)

Qabbalistic Teachings and the Tree of Life by M P Hall (978-1-63118-482-6)

The Sepher Yetzirah and the Qabalah by M P Hall (978-1-63118-481-9)

The Devil in Love by Jacques Cazotte (978–1–63118–499–4)

Crystal Vision Through Crystal Gazing by Frater Achad (978-1-63118-455-0)

The Golden Verses of Pythagoras: Five Translations (978-1-63118-479-6)

Arcane Formulas or Mental Alchemy by W W Atkinson (978-1-63118-459-8)

The Machinery of the Mind by Dion Fortune (978-1-63118-451-2)

The A E Waite Reader: A Selection of Occult Essays (978-1-63118-515-1)

Audio versions are also available on Audible, Amazon and Apple

Other Books in this Series and Related Titles

On the Cave of the Nymphs in the Odyssey by Thomas Taylor (978-1-63118-505-2)

The Poem of Hashish by A Crowley & C Baudelaire (978-1-63118-484-0)

Brothers & Builders by Joseph Fort Newton (978-1-63118-506-9)

The Kabbalah of Masonry & Related Writings by E Levi &c (978-1-63118-453-6)

A Collection of Fiction and Essays by Occult Writers on Supernatural and Metaphysical Subjects by various (978–1–63118–510–6)

Clairvoyance and Psychic Abilities by A Besant &c (978-1-63118-403-1)

Cloud Upon the Sanctuary by Waite & K Eckartshausen (978-1-63118-438-3)

The Hymns of Hermes by G. R. S. Mead (978-1-63118-405-5)

The Secrets of Enoch by Enoch (978-1-63118-449-9)

Masonic and Rosicrucian History by M P Hall & H Voorhis (978-1-63118-486-4)

The Sword of Welleran and Other Stories by Lord Dunsany (978-1-63118-501-4)

The Janeites, The Man Who Would Be King and Other Stories of Freemasonry by Rudyard Kipling (978–1–63118–480–2)

Gnosis of the Mind by G. R. S. Mead (978-1-63118-408-6)

The First and Second Gospels of the Infancy of Jesus Christ by Thomas and James (978-1-63118-415-4)

The Life of Pythagoras by Porphyry (978-1-63118-512-0)

Freemasonry & Catholicism by Max Heindel (978-1-63118-508-3)

The Feminine Occult by various authors (978-1-63118-711-7)

The Influence of Pythagoras on Freemasonry and Other Essays (978-1-63118-404-8)

The Path of Light: A Manual of Maha-Yana Buddhism (978-1-63118-471-0)

Tao Te Ching & Commentary by Lao Tzu & C Johnston (978-1-63118-495-6)

Audio versions are also available on Audible, Amazon and Apple

Table of Contents

Introduction...7

The Camp of Philosophy

Book I: Alchemy...9

Dream of Mr. Bloomfield...11

Book II: Concerning the 7 Planets...24

Theory...27

Practice...33

INTRODUCTION

The word "esoteric" can be difficult to define. Esotericism in general can be seen less as a system of beliefs and more as a category, which encompasses numerous, different systems of beliefs. It's a bit of juxtaposition, since the word "esoteric" indicates something that few people know about, while the term itself broadly covers numerous philosophies, practices, areas of study and belief systems.

In a greater sense, Esotericism acts as a storehouse for secret knowledge, which is often considered ancient (by *tradition, if not by fact)*, passed down from generation to generation, in private. At various times in history, simply possessing the knowledge of some of these subjects, was considered illegal and a jailable offence, if discovered. This usually included such general topics as Alchemy, Pharmacology, Qabalah, Hermeticism, Occultism, Ceremonial Magic, Astrology, Divination, Rosicrucianism and so on. Collectively, these areas of study were often referred to as the esoteric sciences.

Sometimes, the outer garment of a subject isn't esoteric, while what is hidden beneath it, is. As an example, Freemasonry isn't necessarily esoteric by nature (at *least not anymore)*, but certain signs, passwords and handshakes given to the candidate during their initiation, are in fact, esoteric, in the sense that they are hidden from the general public.

Today, in the twenty-first century, such topics are readily available at bookstores across the country, and numerous mainsteam publishers offer beginners guides and coffee-table volumes on many of these subjects, intended for mass appeal. Books like *"The Secret"* have turned previously arcane topics into household knowledge. All that being the case, however, it isn't to say that there still aren't buried secrets to uncover, ancient wisdom being ignored and forgotten mysteries to be explored. In fact, it is often that we are only able to further our own studies by standing on the shoulders of these disappearing giants.

Lamp of Trismegistus is doing its part to help preserve humanity's esoteric history by making some of these classics available to those students who are seeking to unearth the knowledge of these ancient colossi.

So, be sure to check other titles from our *Esoteric Classics* series, as well as our *Occult Fiction, Theosophical Classics, Foundations of Freemasonry Series, Supernatural Fiction, Paranormal Research Series, Studies in Buddhism* and our *Christian Apocrypha Series*. You can also download the audio versions of most of these titles from Amazon, Apple or Audible, for learning on the go.

THE CAMP OF PHILOSOPHY

The compendiary of the noble science of alchemy compiled by Mr Willm Blomefeild philosopher & bacheler of phisick admitted by king Henry the 8th of most famous memory. Anno Domini 1557

1

When Phebus was entered the signe of the ramm,
In the month of march when all Doth springe,
Lying in my bed, an old man to me came.
Laying his hand on my buysy head slumbringe,
"I am," he said, "Tyme, producer of cunninge.
Awake & rise, prepare thy selfe quickly;
My entent is to bring thee to [the Campe of] philosophy.

2

"Bloomes & blossomes plentiful in that feild
Bynn pleasantly flourishinge, vernant with collers gay.
Liuely water fountaines, eke beastes both tame & wild
Ouershadowed with trees fruitful, & on euery spray
Melodiously singinge, the birdes doe sitt & say:
'Father, sonn, & holy ghoste, to one god [in] persons three;
Impery & honor be to the holy trinitye.'"

3

Lo! thus when he had said, I arose swiftly,
Doeing on my clothes in haste with agility.
Towardes the camp, wee went, of philosophi,
The wonderful sightes there for to see.
To a large greate gate, father tyme first brought me,
Which closed was; then he to me saide,
"Each thing his time hath; be thou nothing Dismaied."

4

The great admiracion I tooke into my selue,
With sore & huge perturbacions of minde,
Beholdinge the gate fastned with lockes twelue.
I fantasied but smalle that time should be my freind.
"Why studiest thou, man," quoth he; "art thou blind?"
With a rodd he touched me, whereat I Did Downe fall
Into a straunge sleepe, & In a Dreame he showed me all.

The Dreame of Mr Blomefeild

5

Audite somnium meum quod vidi.
The Mt yeere of Christ, D L & seuen,
In the month of march, asleep as I did lye,
Late in the night, of the clocke about eleuen,
In spiritu rapt I was, soodenly into heauen;
Where I saw sittinge in most glorious maiesty
Three beholding, I adored but one in deitye:

6

A Spirit incircumscript with burninge heate incombustible;
Light of brightnes permanent, as fountaine of all light;
Three knit in one, with glory incomprehensible,
Which to behold I had a greate Delighte.
This trulye [to attayne] surmounted my might;
But a voice from that glorious brightnes to me saide,
"I am one god of Immeasurable maiesty: [be not afraide]."

7

In this vision so cleare, that it selfe did so extend
With a voice most pleasant, being three & one,
Pearsed my minde, & taught me to comprehende
The darke sayinges of philosophers each one:
The altitude, latitude & profundity of the stone
To be three in substance & one in essence,
A most heauenly treasure procreate by quintessence.

8

The studied I what quintessence should be;
Of visible thinges apparant to the eye
The fifth being, even a straunge privity
In euery substance resting invisibly.
The invisible godheade is the same, thought I,
Prime cause of beinge & the prime essence,
And of this macrocosm the most suffren quintessence.

9

This is the heauenly and secret potencyall
That Devided is, & resteth indivisible
In [all] thinges animall, vigitall, & minerall;
Whose vertue in them, & strength, is invisible.
From god it cometh, & god maketh it sencible
To some preelect; to other doth it denay.
As I sate thus museinge, a voice to me did say:

10

"Study thou no more of my being, but stedfastly
Beleeue this trinity equally knit in one.
Further of my Secretes to muse is but folly,
Passing thy capassity, & all human reason."
The heauens closed vp againe in that season.
Then father Tyme set me at the gate,
And Deliuered me a key to enter in thereat:

11

The key of knowledge & excellent Science,
Whereby all secretes of philosophi are reserate:
The Secretes of nature sought out by Diligence,
Voidinge fables envious of fooles inveterate:
With recipe & Decipe, this science is violate.
Therefore [to me] this key he did Dispose,
The secretes of this art to open & Disclose.

12

This said father Tyme, this key when he mee tooke:
"Vnlock," quoth he, "this gate by thy selue."
And then vpon him sorrowfully Did I looke,
Saying that one key vndoe could not lockes twelue.
"Whose axe is sure," quoth he, "both the head & helue,
Hold will together till the tree Downe fall.
So open thou the first locke, & thou hast opened all."

13

"What is this first locke named, tell me then,
I Pray thee," said I, "and what shall I it call?"
"It is," quoth he, "the secret of all the wise men,
Chaos; in the bodies called the first originall,
Prima materia, our mercury, our menstruall,
Our vitrioll, our sulphur, our lunary most of price.
Put the key in the locke, & it will open with a trice.

14

Then the key of knowledge buysily I tooke in hand,
And began to search the hollownes of the locke;
The wardes thereof I scare did vnderstand,
So craftily conveid they were in their stocke.
I proued euery way; at the last I did vnlocke
The crafty ginnes thus made for the nonce,
And with it, the other lockes fell open all at once.

15

At this gate opening, euen in the entry
A number of philosophers in the face I mett,
Workeing all one way the secretes of philosophy
Vpon Chaos Darke, that amongst them was sett.
Sober men of liueing, peaceable & quiet,
They buysily Disputed de materia prima,
Reiecting cleane away simul stulta et friuola.

16

Heere I saw the father of philosophers, Hermes.
Heere I saw Aristotle with cheere most Iocunde.
Heere I saw Morien & Senior in turba more & lesse;
Geber, [Democritus], Albert, Bacon, & Ramond;
The monke, & the chanon of Bridleington so profound;
Workeing most soberly, who said vnto me:
"Beware though beleeue not all that thou dost see,

17

"But if thou wilt enter this camp of philosophy,
With thee take time to guide thee in the way;
For by pathes & broade waies, Deep vallyes & hils high
Here shalt thou finde with sightes pleasant & gay.
Some thou shalt finde which vnto thee shall say,
'Recipe this & that,' & with a thowsand thinges more
Decipe thy selfe & other[s] as they haue done before."

18

Then father Tyme & I by fauour of these men,
Such sightes to see, passed foorth toward the campe
Where wee met Disguised philosophers ten,
With porfiries & morters, ready to grind & stamp;
Their heades shakeing, their hands full of the cramp;
Some lame [with] spasums, some febull, wann, & blind,
With arsneck & sulphur, to this art most vnkind.

19

These were Broke the preste & yorke in cotes gay,
Which robbed king henry of a million of gold;
Martin pery, mayre, & thomas De Lahaye,
Saying that the king they greatly enrich would.
They wispered in his eare, & this tale him told:
"Wee will worke for your highnes the Elixer vite,
A princely worke called opus regale."

20

Then brought they in the vicar of Maldon
With his lyon greene, that most royall secret,
Richard record & little Master Edon
(Their mettals by corrosiue[s] to calcinate & fret);
Hugh oldcastle & Sir Robert greene with them mett,
Rosting & broileinge all thinges out of kinde,
Like philosophers left off with loss in the end.

21

Yet brought they [forth] thinges beautifull to sight,
Deluding the king thus from day to day;
With copper cytrinate for the red, and albefied [for] the white,
And with mercury rubified in a glass full gay.
But at the last, in the fire, it went away.
All this was because they neuer knew the verity
Of altitude, latitude, & profunditye.

22

Thence father Tyme brought me to a wildernes,
Into a thicket haueing by pathes many [a one].
Steps & footinges I saw there more & lesse,
Wherein the foresaid men had wandered & gone.
There I saw Marcasites, minerals, & many a stone,
As yrides, talke, & alom lay digged from the ground,
The mines of leade & Iron that they had out fownde.

23

No marvell I trow, though they were much set by,
That with so greate riches could [endue] a kinge.
So many sundry waies to fill vp his treasurie
With filthy matter, great charges in to bring:
The very next way a prince to bring to begginge,
And make a noble realme & common wealth decay.
These are royall philosophers the cleane contrary way.

24

From thence foorth I went, Tyme beinge my guide,
Through a greene wood where birdes sang clearly,
Tyll wee came to a feild, pleasant, large, & wide,
Which he said was called the camp of philosophy.
There downe we sate, to heere the sweete harmony
Of the diuers birdes in their sweete notes singinge,
And to receiue the flauour of the flowers springinge.

25

Heere Iuno, heere pallas, heere Apollo doe Dwell;
Heere true philosophers take their dwelling place.
Heere duly the muses nine drinck of pirenes well.
No bosting broyler heere the art can deface.
Heere lady philosophi hath her royall palace,
Holding her court in her high consistory,
Sitting with her councelers most famous of memory.

26

Thus one said vnto me (an ancient man was he),
Declareing [forth] the matter of the stone,
Saying that he was sent thither to comfort me,
And of his religion for to chuse me to be one.
A cloth of tyssew he had him vpon,
Verged aboute with pearles of collers fresh & gay.
He proceeded with his taile, & againe thus did say:

27

"Heere all occult secretes of Nature knowne are;
Heere all the elementes from thinges are drawne out.
Heere fire, air, & water in earth are knit together;
Heere all our secret worke is truly brought aboute.
Heere you must learne in thy busines to be stout:
Night & day thou must tend thy work buysily,
Haueing constant pacience & neuer to be weary."

28

As we sate talkeing by the riuers running cleere,
I cast my eye aside, & there I did behold
A lady most excellent, sitting in her arbor,
Which clothed was in a robe of fine gold,
Set about with stones & pearles many fold.
Then asked I father Tyme what hee should be.
"Lady philosophy," quoth he, "most excellent of beauty."

29

Then I was stricken with an ardent avidity
The place to approche to, where I saw that sight.
I rose vp to walk, & the other two went before me
Against the arbor, till I came foorth right.
Then we all three, humbly as we might,
Bowed down our selues to her with humility,
With greate admiracion extolling her felicity.

30

Shee shewed her selue both gentill & benigne:
Her gesture & countenace gladdid our cominge.
From her seate imperiall, shee did her selfe incline,
As a lady loueing perfect wisedome & cunninge.
Her goodly poems her beauty was surmountinge:
Her speech was decorate with such auriate sentence,
Far above excelling famous tullye's eloquence.

31

The father tyme vnto the Lady saide,
"Pleaseth your highnes this poore man to heere,
Him to assist with your most gracious aide?"
Then she commanded him with me to draw neere.
"Son," said the lady, "be thou of good cheere.
Admitted thou shalt be amongst greate & smale,
A disciple to be of my secretes all."

32

Then she committed me vnto Ramon Lully,
Commanding him my simplenes to instructe,
And in her secretes to induce me fully:
Into her priuy garden, for to be my conducte.
First into a towre, most beautifull constructe,
Father Ramond brought me, & thence immediately
He led me to her garden, planted most deliciously.

33

Among the faire trees, one tree in especiall,
Most vernant & pleasant, appeared to my sight.
A name inscribed, "the tree philosophical,"
Which to behold I had great delight.
Then to philosophy my troth I plight,
Her maiesty to serue, & to take greate paine,
The fruites of that tree with Ramond to attaine.

34

Then Raymonde shewed me budes fiftene
Spring of the tree, & fruites fiftene mo.
"Of the which," said he, "proceedeth that wee doe mean,
That all philosophers couet to attaine to,
The blessed stone, one in number & no mo:
Our great Elixer most high of price,
Our azoc, our Adrope, our basilicke, our cockatrice.

35

"This is our antimony & our red leade,
Gloriously shineing as Phebus at midday.
This is our crowne of glory & Diadem of our head
Whose beames resplendent shall neuer fade away.
Who attaineth this treasure never can decay:
It is a Iewell so abundant & excellent,
That one graine will endure euer to be permanent.

36

"I leave thee heere now, our secretes to attaine.
Look that thou earnestly my counsell doe ensue:
There needes no blowing at the cole be, nore paine,
But at thine owne ease here maist thou continue.
Old, Ancient writers beleeue which are true,
And they shall thee learne to pass it to bringe.
Beware therefore of many, & hold thee to one thinge.

37

"This one thing is nought els but the lyon greene,
[Which] some fooles imagine to be vitrioll roman.
It is not that thing that the philosophers meane,
For nothing to vs any corosiue doe pertaine.
Vnderstand, therefore, or else thy hand refraine
From this hard science, lest you doe worke amiss.
For I will tell the truth; marke now what it is:

38

"Greene of collor our lyon is not truly,
But vernant & greene, euermore endurringe.
In his most bitternes of death, he is liuely;
In the burning fire he is euermore springinge.
Therefore the Salamander, by the fire liueing,
Some men doth him call, & some another name:
The mettalline menstruall, it is euen the same.

39

"Some call it allso a substance exuberate.
Some call it mercury of mettalline essence;
Some, limus deserti, from his body evacuate;
Some, the eagle flyinge from the north with violence.
Some call it a tode for his great vehemence.
But few or none at all doe name it in his kind:
It is a priuy quintessence; keepe it well in minde.

40

"This is not in sight, but resteth invisible
Tyll he be forced out of Chaos darke,
Wher he remaineth euer indiuisible.
And yet in him is foundacion of our worke;
In our lead it is, so that thou it marke:
Dryue it out of him, so out of all other.
I can tell thee no better if thou were my brother.

41

"This Chaos Darke the mettals I doe call,
Because as in a prison it resteth them within.
The secret of nature they keepe in thrall
Which by a meane wee doe out twine;
The workeing whereof the easlier to begin,
Lift vp thy head and looke vpon the heauen,
And I will learn thee truly to know the planetes seven.

finis primi libri

The Second Booke concerninge the 7 planetes

42

"Saturne malivolous, to this art hath respect,
Of whom wee draw a quintessence excellent.
Vnto our mastery him selfe he doth converte,
Vnited in quality, & allso made equipolent
In strength & vertue. Who lust to be diligent
Shall find that wee seeke an heavenly treasure,
And a precious Iewell that euer shall endure.

43

"Iubiter the gentill, indewed with azure blew,
Examinate by iustice, Declareth true Iudgment;
Altering his colour euer fresh & new,
In his occult nature to this art is convenient;
To philosophi is seruiable & allso obedient,
Ioyned with lunary after his owne kinde
Conteneth this art & leaueth nothing behinde.

44

"Mars that is martiall in citty and in towne,
Ferce in battle, full of debate & strife,
A noble warryour & famous of renowne,
With fire & sword defendeth his owne life.
He stayneth with blood, & slayeth with a knife
All spirites & bodies, his artes bee so bold.
The hartes of all other he winneth with gold.

45

"The Sonn most gloriously shininge is prepotent
Aboue all the other faire planetes seven;
Shedding his light to them all indifferent.
WIth his golden beames & glistering stevyn,
He lighteneth the earth & the firmament of heaven.
Who can him Dissolue, & draw out his quintessence,
Vnto all other planetes he shall giue influence.

46

"Lady venus, of loue the fayre goddesse,
With her Sonn cupid appertaineth to this art.
To the loue of the sonn when she Doth her dresse,
With her dart of loue striketh him to the hart.
Ioyned to his seede, of his substance she taketh part.
Her selue she endeweth with excellent tissew,
Her corrupt nature [when she doth renewe].

47

"Mercury this seeing, beginneth to be fugitiue.
With his rod of enchantment little Doth prevaile:
Taken often prisoner, himselfe doth reviue,
Till he be snarled with the Dragon's taile;
Then Doth he on an hard coate of maile,
Sodered together with the Sunn & the moone:
Then he is mastered & his enchantment Done.

48

"The moone, that is called the lesser [luminarie],
Wife to phebus, shining by night
To other giueth her garment; through her orbe lunary
From the north to the south shineth full bright.
If ye for her doe seeke, shee hideth from your sight,
But by fair entreaty she is wonn at the last:
With azoc & fire, the whole mastery thou hast.

49

"The mastery thou gettest not of these planetes seven,
But by a misty meaninge, known onely vnto vs.
Bring them first to hell & afterward to heauen;
Betwixt life & Death them you must Discus.
Therefore I counsaile thee, see that you worke thus:
Solue & seperate them, sublyme, fix, & congeale;
Then hast thou all, therefore doe as I thee tell.

50

"Dissolue not with corosiue nor vse seperation
With vehemence of fire, as multipliers doe vse;
Nor to the glas topp make you sublimacion.
Such waies inordinate, philosophers refuse.
Their sayinges follow & wisely them pervse;
Then shalt thou not thy selfe ludely Delude
In this godly science. Adew; thus I conclude."

per me Wll. Blomefild

Incipit theorica per Wll Blomefild

51

[We] intend now, through grace Devine,
In few wordes of Chaos to write;
Light from darknes to cause foorth to shine,
Long before hidden, as I shall recyte.
In euery thing vnknown, it is requisite
A secret to search out which is invisible,
Materiall of our mastery, a substance invincible.

52

Because I should not seeme to [disclose]
Long hidden treasure vnto me committed
Of my lord god, therefore plaine of Chaos
My purpose shalbe there of to be acquited.
For Daungerous burdens are not easily lighted.
In faith, therefore, my selfe I shall endeuor
Lightly to Discharge me, before god for euer.

53

Devoutly, therefore, o lord vnto thee I call:
Send me thy grace to make explanacion
Of Chaos. For thou art opener of secretes all,
Which euer art ready to heare the exclamacion
Of thy meeke servantes, which with harty humiliacion
To thee doe apply: send me now thy grace,
Of thy secretes to write in due order, time, & place.

54

Chaos is no more to say (this is doubtelesse,
As Ovid witnesseth in his metamorphosyn)
But a certaine rude substance, indigestaque moles,
Haueing diuers natures resting it within,
Which with the contrarie, wee may out twine
By philosopher's arte. Who so the feate doth know,
The fower elementes from Chaos can out [drawe].

55

This Chaos, as all thinges, hath Dimencions three,
Which well considered shall follow the effect:
That is, altitude, latitude, & profunditye,
By the which three all the matter is [detect].
Vnto these dimencions who hath not a respect
Shall neuer Devide this Chaos in his kinde,
But after his labour, shall find fraud in the end.

56

Chaos is to us the vine tree, white & red.
Chaos is each beest, fowle, & fish in his kinde.
Chaos is the ore & mine of tinn & leade,
Of gold and siluer that we doe out finde,
Iron & Copper, which thinges doe binde
And hold our sight & wittes to them bounde;
The secret hidd in them, that wee ne vnderstand.

57

[Out of this mistie] Chaos, the philosophers expert
Do a substance out draw, called a quintessence,
Craftely deviding the fower elementes by art,
With greate wisedome, study, & dilegence.
The which high secret hath a diuine influence
That is supernaturall (of fooles thought impossible),
An oyle or much like, called incombustible.

58

The mastery of this plainly to shew thee,
In forme here after I will it Declare,
Setting foorth heere the philosopher's tree,
Wherein the whole art now I shall compare.
In this faire tree [sixteene] fruites are,
More pretious then gold in thy stomacke to digest.
Put thy hand therto, & taste of the best.

59

And leste the fault should imputed be
In me or in other that of this art do write,
I set before thee the true figure of the tree,
Wherein orderly this art I will recyte.
Vnderstand my sentence that thou maist worke right,
Considering as I said that Chaos is all thing
That we begin of, the true way of workinge.

60

Put case thy Chaos be animall, vigetall, or minerall;
Let reason guide thee to worke after the same.
If thou workest out of kind, then loosest thou all;
For nature with nature ioyeth & maketh true game.
Worke animall with his kind, & keep thee out of blame;
Vigetall & minerall in their order Dew,
Then shalt thou be taken for a philosopher trew.

61

When thou hast fownde what it is indeede,
Then knowest thou thy forme, what by reason it must be.
Search it wittyly & Draw from him his seede.
There is then thy altitude superficiall to see;
The latitude anon shall appeare: beleeue mee.
When thou hast Deuided the elementes asunder,
Then the profundity amongest them [lyeth] hid vnder.

62

Here is materia prima et corpus confusum,
But not yet the matter which philosophers Doe treate.
Yet the one conteineth the other in somme,
For forma, materia, [et] corpus together are knite.
With the menstruall water thou must them frett,
That the body first be finely calcinate,
After dissolued & purely euacuate.

63

Then is he the trew mercury of philosophers,
Vnto the mastry apt, needful, & serviable.
More of this thing I need not much rehearse,
For this is all the secret most commendable.
Materia prima it is called multiplicable,
The which by art must be exuberate:
Then is it the matter that mettals were of generate.

64

Sulphur of nature, & not that which is common,
Of mettals must be made if that thou wilt speede;
Which will turn [them] to his kind euery each one.
His tincture into them abroad he will spreade.
It will fix mercury common at thy neede,
And make him apt, true tincture to receiue.
Worke as I haue told thee, & it shall not thee deceiue.

65

Then of Sunn & moone make your oile incombustible
With mercury vegitable or els with lunary.
Incerate therewith, & make thy sulphur possible
To abide the fire, & allso thy mercury
Be fixt & flowinge. Then hast thou wrought truly,
And so hast thou made a worke for the nonce,
And gotten a precious stone of all stones.

66

Fix it vp now with perfect Decoction,
And that with easy fire & not vehement,
For fear of induracion or vitrificacion,
Lest you loose all & thy labour be mispent.
With eight Daies & nightes this stone is sufficient:
The greate Elixer, most high of price,
Which Ramond calleth his basilicke & cockatrise.

67

To this excellent worke greate cost neede not to be:
Many glasses or pots about it to breake.
One glas, one furnace, & no mo of necessity;
Who mo doth spoile, his wittes are but weake.
All this is stilled in a limbecke with a beacke
(As touching the order of distillacions),
And with a blind head in the same for solucions.

68

In this thy mercury taketh his true kinde.
In this he is brought to multiplication.
In this made he is Sulphur: beare it in mind.
Tincture here in he taketh, & inceration.
In this the stone is brought to his perfect creacion,
In one glas, one thing, one fire, & no moe.
This worke is complete: Da gloriam deo.

finis theorica per Wll. B.

Incipit Practica: per Wll. Blomefild

69

Wee haue declared sufficiently the theoricke,
In wordes misticall makeing Declaration.
Let vs now proceede plaine with the practicke,
Largely of the matter to make explanacion.
I will, therefore, that thou marke well my narracion,
As true disciples my doctrine ye attend:
My testament & last will to you I doe commend.

70

Be you holy, therefore, sober, honest, & meeke.
Loue god & your neighbor; to the poore be not vnkinde.
Ouercome sathan; god's glory see you seeke.
My sonn, be gentle to all men, as a freind;
Fatherles & widdowes haue euer in thy minde.
Innocentes loue as brothers; the wicked Doe eschew.
Let falsehood & flattery goe, lest that thou it rew.

71

Devoutely serue god, call Daily for his grace.
Worship him in spirrit, with hart contryte & pure;
In no wise let sathan thy prayers deface.
Looke thou be stedfast in faith & trust most sure.
Long sufference & patience with thee let long endure;
In all aduersitye be gentle in thy hart
Against thy foe: so shalt thou him convert.

72

Most hartily therefore, o lord, to thee I call,
Beseeching thee to ayd me with thy heauenly grace.
Louingly thy spirit vpon me let Down fall,
Ouershadowing me that I at no tyme trespas.
My lord & my god, graunt me to purchase
Full knowledge of thy secretes, with thy mercy to winn.
Intending the truth, this practice I beginn.

73

Listen now, my Sonn, & thy eares encline.
Delight haue thou to learne this practice, sage and true.
Attend my sayinges & note well this Discipline,
These rules following: Doe as [it] doth ensue:
This labor once begun, thou must it Continue
Without teadious sluggerdy & slothfull wearynes;
So shalt thou thereby acquire to thee right riches.

74

In the name of God, this secret to attaine,
Ioyne thou in one body with a perfect vnity
First the red man & the white woman, these twaine.
One of the man's substance, & of the woman's three;
By liquifaction together ioyned they must be:
The which coniunction is called Diptatyue,
That is made betweene man & wife.

75

Then after that they be one body made,
With the sharp teeth of a Dragon finely
Bring them to dust. The next must be had:
The true proportion of that dust truly
In a true ballance, waying it equally
With three times as much of the firy dragon fell,
Mixing all together: then hast thou done well.

76

Thy substance together thus proporcionate,
Put into a bed of glas with a bottome large & round,
There in due time to dye, & be regenerate
Into a new nature: three natures in one bound.
Then be thou glad that euer thou it found,
For this is the Iewell that shall stand thee most in stead,
The crowne of glory & diademe of thy head.

77

When thou hast thus mixed thy matter as is said,
Stop well thy glas, that the dragon goe not owt;
For he is so subtill that if he be ouerlayde
With fyre vnnaturall (I put thee owt of dowbte),
For to escape he wyll search all abowte.
Therefore with gentyll fyre, looke that thou kepe [it] in:
So shalt thou of him the whole maistry wynne.

78

The whole maistery here of, Duly to fullfill,
Set thy glas & matter vpon the athanor,
One furnace called the philosopher's Dunghill.
With a temperate heate workeing euermore,
Night & day continually haue fuell in store,
Or turfe, or saw Dust, or dry chipped segges,
That the heate be equipolent to the henn vpon her eggs.

79

Such heate continuall, looke that it doth not lacke.
Forty Dayes long for their perfect vnition
In them is made, for first it turneth blacke.
This colour betokeneth the right putrifaction.
This is the beginning of perfect conception
Of your infant into a new generacion:
A most precious Iewell for our great consolation.

80

Forty dayes then more, thy matter shall turne white
And cleere as pearles, which is a declaracion
Of voideing away of his cloudes, darke, & night.
This sheweth our infante's organisacion,
Our white elixer, most cleere in his carnacion.
From white vnto all coloures without faile,
Like to the rainbow or to the peacocke's taile.

81

So foorth augment thy fire continually;
Vnder thy matter easely they must be fedd.
Till those colours begon, rule it wisely;
For soone after appeareth yellow, the [messenger] to red.
When that is come, then hast thou well sped,
And hast brought forth a stone of price,
Which raymond calleth his basylicke & cockatrice.

82

Then forty Daies to take his whole fixation:
Let it so stand in heate most temperate,
That in that time you spare the firmentation
To encrease him withall. That it be not violate,
Beware of fire & water, for that will it suffocate.
Take one to an hundreth vnto this confection,
And vpon crude mercury make thy proiection.

83

One of the stone, I meane, vpon an hundreth fold
(After the first & second right fermentation)
Of mercury crude, turneth it to fine gold:
As fine & as good, as naturall in ponderacion
(The stone is so vehement in his penetracion);
Fixt & fusible, as the goldsmithe's sowder is.
Worke as I haue said, & you cannot Doe amisse.

84

Now giue thankes to the blessed trinity
For the benefit of this pretious stone,
That with his grace so much hath lightened thee,
Him for to know, being three [in] one.
Hold vp thy handes to his heauenly throne;
To his maiesty let vs sing hosanna:
Altissimo Deo sit honor et gloria.

Amen. W.B.

www.ingramcontent.com/pod-product-compliance
Lightning Source LLC
LaVergne TN
LVHW041503070426
835507LV00009B/779